foreword

This book has been specially compiled by Angus Council from a selection o
of "Wishes" received from the children of Angus who were asked to expr
about the future in the run up to the new Millennium.

It provides a fascinating insight not only into our social history, but into the minds of children aged 5 - 14 as they tell us the most important things in their lives in the immediate future and **for the 21st Century, whether global or personal.**

Ashton (5yr)

All profits from the sale of this book will be donated to CHILDREN 1ST
(Royal Scottish Society for Prevention of Cruelty to Children)

(Registered Charity No. SC 016092).

health

I want my family to be well looked after. Eilidh 8

My Wish for the year 2000 is that the people in the poor countries could have clean water and food. Axel Class 3/4

My wish for the Millennium is that there will be more medicine so that fewer people die.

Carina age 9

My wish is to ban fags because my Grandpa died of cancer.

Michael 8

I wish that everyone in the whole world would stop smoking. Joanne 7

I Wish that people would have homes and clean water and food and good clothes to wear

Hannah 9 year old

Hannah 9

A cure for all deadly diseases globalwide

Ryan (11)

My wish for the millennium is that more people can be cured from an illness other than killed from an illness.

Erin 9yr.

I WISH THERE WOULD BE A CURE FOR AIDS

FRASER AGE 13

I wish blind people will have more guide dogs.

Kerry 7

I wish that there were cures to diseases which don't have cures.
Fraser

I wish nobody died. PS Please can you make my wish come true.
Emily 7

I wish I could work with my granda and grow lots of tatties. Tatties help you grow big.
Gordie age 4

I wish to live till I am 100.
Amy Age 10

My millennium Wish

I wish that everyone who is in heaven would come down from heaven.
Sally age 6

Scotland

I wish there was peace in the world and Scotland would win the World Cup.
Rory 11

My best wish for the year 2000 is that someone could bring William Wallace back.
David 10

I wish that there would be lower taxes.
Joanna 12

My wish for the Millennium is for Scotland to be the best in health rather than the worst - so don't smoke and we will be more healthy.
Karis 11

I wish I was the King of Scotland

teacher
miss simpson

Gary C
class P5
age 9

family

I wish mums would stop shouting.

Claire 7

I wish my gran could get her teeth fixed so she will be happy.

April 5

My wish for the Millennium is so that I can see my Dad every day because at the moment he works so hard that he doesn't come home until late.

Robyn P5

I wish families would not split up.

John

I wish that grandad could get some hairspray.
Sasha 4

I wish everyone had a mum and dad.
Darren 4

kids!

I wish everyone had a beautiful garden. Christopher age 5

I wish that everything would go right!
Jonathan 7

More things to do for teenagers.
Kevin 14

I wish that I could write things.
Jamie

Kenneth 13

I wish that I cold sppel propela.

Sory about speeling miztakes

I wish I could hold a butterfly.

Lori-Jo 5

I wish that teenagers were treated as equals. It's only a small minority which gets into trouble, so why should we all be looked down on?

Nicki 13

I wish there could be a children's 'Who wants to be a millionaire' show.

Drew 8 and pic by Steven 10

..children with difficulties in life should have a better chance.

Fraser 9

I wish I was a chocolate taster.
Jordan 8

I wish for a scary spider.
Brian 5

I wish the park had a bumpy chute.
Cally 6

I wish the world was made of chocolate.
Val 12

I wish I can get to the end of the rainbow.
Nicola Age 8

I wish I had a new coat because my Postman Pat ripped

Kerri 6yrs

...a time machine to see into the future.

Liam 8

I wish I was a parrot.

David 8

I wish I passed swimming Lessons just on one day

Angus 6yrs

I wish that it was sunny evesy day

Kanene
Age 5

My millennium wish is that it would be Friday every day!!!

Jack 12

I wish for a machine which will tell you the answers to all your questions

Laura

I wish that if I put money in the ground it would make a money tree.

Sean 7

the world

I wish everyone was polite.
Ashton 5

I wish the world was more calm.
Hayley 10

My wish for the new millennium is for everybody

2000 MILLENNIUM

in the world to get enough food to live.
AGE 10 Arron

I wish that more animals, trees and people could have safe places to live.

Jayne

I wish that all child abuse would stop!
Katy 9

I wish that some day we would find out if there is life on any other planet in the universe.

Jordan
10 Years old

My millennium wish is that the people in Romania will have a happy life.

Carrie P6

...that all the refugees in Kosovo get the things that people have sent them.

Laura 10

...for nobody in the world to be poor.

Philip 11

I wish rich people would donate to the poor.

Sam 9

My wish for the Millennium is to respect people for what they are. **Michaela 11**

I wish the whole world would be fair, kind and nice

DARRYL AGE—8

I wish everyone had enough money to buy things.

Jamie Watson (6)

My millennium wish would be that each child over 7 years old must give up one christmas present and get the money for it in its place, and with this money you and your friends could add their money and then sponsor a child in a poor country.

Luke 10

I wish for everyone to have a home.

MICHAEL 7

I wish the world would never blow up.

Matthew 8

I wish that my mum and I win the lottery and help all the very poor people all over the world.

Craig P5/6

I wish that it would rain money and nobody would be poor.

Adam Age 8

I wish everyone would be treated as equals whether you are black, white or yellow with blue dots.

Faye 13

I wish the world had no more earthquakes.

James 8

animals

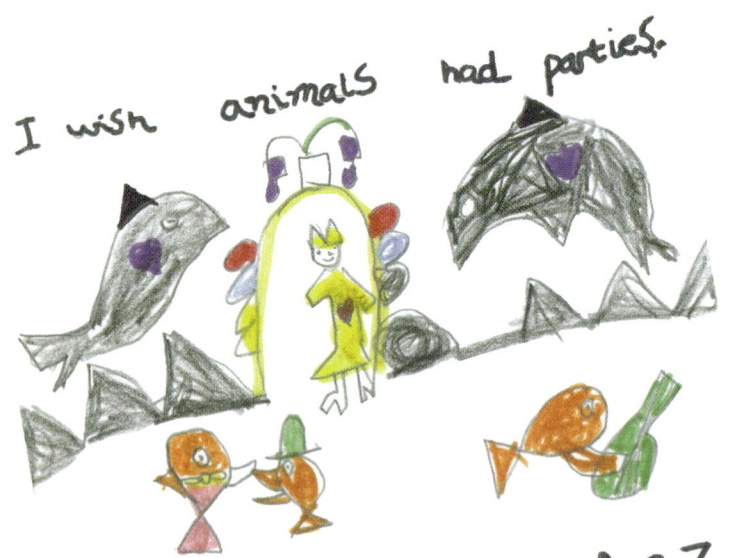

I wish animals had parties.

By Susan Age 7

I wish that anything living should be helped - not harmed.

ASHLEIGH 10yr.

I'd like us to have magical powers so we could listen to the animals.

Tze-Yan 13

I wish that all creatures are safe

Ross 7

I WISH: People would be kind to animals

By Stephanie

age 10

I wish animals were treated like humans.

Name: Christopher   age: 9

My wish for the Millennium is that there are no more poachers. Laura 11

I wish that my puppy would always stay little because it looks cute. Jenna 8

I wish tigers will be safe for a long time.

FIONA 10

peace in our time

I wish there were no more wars.

Age 7 Callum

...peace in East Timor.
Sarah 9

I wish for peace in Ireland.
Lisa 13

I hope that there will be peace everywhere and no more wars.
Name Greig
Age 11 years old

I wish people would stop trying to be more powerful than other people.
Jake 8

My Millennium wish is that people would forget their petty differences and get along with each other.

Gordon   age 11

My wish for the year 2000 is there will be no war and all the nations will come together and be as one.
by Layla
Age 12 Class 1.7

I wish that all the people in the world could listen more carefully.
Craig

I wish that everyone had friends.

Paula Age 6

I wish guns would stop being made.

Iain 8

I wish that racism was stopped all over the world

Chelsea 10

I wish the wars in Northern Ireland would stop and the world will be a better place.

Gary 9

I wish that people would care more for each other.

Fiona 8

I wish people would stop fighting.

Michaela Ace

My wish that there will be no falling out or bullying

Please!

Sarah 10 yrs

My Millennium wish is to have peace in the world because we only live once. Jack 11

environment

I wish ships would not sink.
Amy Age 8

I wish the trains never crashed.
Steven 9

I wish people would use buses instead of cars.
Cathleen 13

MY WISH FOR THE MILLENNIUM

Why don't you stop thinking about yourself and do something for the earth you live on.

Ben (11)

I wish we could build new robots to fix the ozone layer.
Greg, Cub Scouts

I wish it was always sunny.
Stuart 5

I wish my mum would stop throwing away her glass bottles so I could put them in the recycling bin.
Leanne 10

I wish that people would stop making the world A tip Tidy up!!! by Derek Age 8

I wish this would stop! and this would start!

Christopher

My Millennium Wish is that people won't cut down rainforests 2000

Joanne 10 years old

Angus

I wish for a new football stadium for Arbroath FC.
Jaime 13

I wish that Arbroath sports centre would invent a bike that you did not have to peddle.
Darren 12

I wish people wouldn't litter our town.
Stephen 10

I wish that the millenium dome was in Forfar
Andrew age 10 P6/7

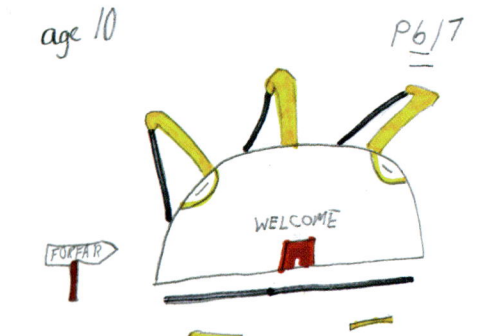

My wish for the millennium is to help my town.
Keri 11

CAROLINE
PRESERVE* OUR TOWN FOR THE FUTURE! '99

I wish there was a shopping centre in Forfar.
Laura 10

I wish that Brechin could have their own recycling centre.
Sharyn 10

I wish that Carnoustie will be a safer place to live. *Drew 8*

school

I wish the world would stop just for a few days to let me catch up.

Jim Anderson, Director of Education

I Wish that We Could have Something like a time-machine So I Could learn my history more easily

Sarah Aged 11

I wish the Scottish Parliament said the schools should have more holidays.

Sarah 10

I wish that children rules the world and we did not get any homework.

Philip 9

I wish that they invented robots to do your work at school

Age 10 BY Paul

I wish that the school would be quiet. Jillian 7

and finally...

I wish for the year 2000 to be the best ever. Gavin 8

2000 MILLENNIUM

Cheers to a happy millennium, keep smiling, keep joyful, keep laughing.
Alison 10